Lewis Helfand

THE WRIGHT BROTHERS

CAMPFIRE™

KALYANI NAVYUG MEDIA PVT. LTD.
New Delhi

THE WRIGHT BROTHERS

Sitting around the Campfire, telling the story, were:

AUTHOR **LEWIS HELFAND**
ILLUSTRATOR **SANKHA BANERJEE**
COLORIST **PRASHANT K. G.**
LETTERER **BHAVNATH CHAUDHARY**
EDITORS **SUPARNA DEB & EMAN CHOWDHARY**
EDITOR (INFORMATIVE CONTENT) **RASHMI MENON**
PRODUCTION CONTROLLER **VISHAL SHARMA**
ART DIRECTOR **RAJESH NAGULAKONDA**
COVER ART **SANKHA BANERJEE & JAYAKRISHNAN K. P.**
DESIGNER **JAYAKRISHNAN K. P.**

CAMPFIRE™

www.campfire.co.in

Published by Kalyani Navyug Media Pvt. Ltd.
101 C, Shiv House, Hari Nagar Ashram, New Delhi 110014, India
www.campfire.co.in
ISBN: 978-93-80028-46-0

Printed in India at Rave India

ABOUT THE AUTHOR

Lewis Helfand was born on April 27, 1978 in Philadelphia and grew up in nearby Narberth, Pennsylvania. Although interested in cartoons and animation from a young age, by the time he was twelve, Lewis's focus had turned to writing. After completing high school, he remained in the Philadelphia area with the intention of pursuing a degree in English.

Four years later, with a political science degree and a passion for comic books, Lewis began working for local publishers by proofreading books and newspaper articles. By the age of twenty-four, Lewis had been editing phonebooks for a year and a half and felt no closer to his lifelong goal of writing comic books. One day he decided to quit his job.

Lewis then spent the next two months working day and night to write and draw his first comic book, *Wasted Minute*, the story of a world without crime where superheroes are forced to work regular jobs. To cover the cost of self-publishing, he began working odd jobs in offices and restaurants and started exhibiting at local comic-book conventions. With the first issue well received, he was soon collaborating with other artists and released four more issues over the next few years.

At the same time, Lewis continues to work outside the field of comic books as a freelance writer and reporter for a number of national print and online publications. He has covered everything from sports and travel to politics and culture for magazines such as *Renaissance*, *American Health and Fitness*, and *Computer Bits*.

ORVILLE WRIGHT

WILBUR WRIGHT

KATHARINE WRIGHT

GLENN CURTISS

OCTAVE CHANUTE

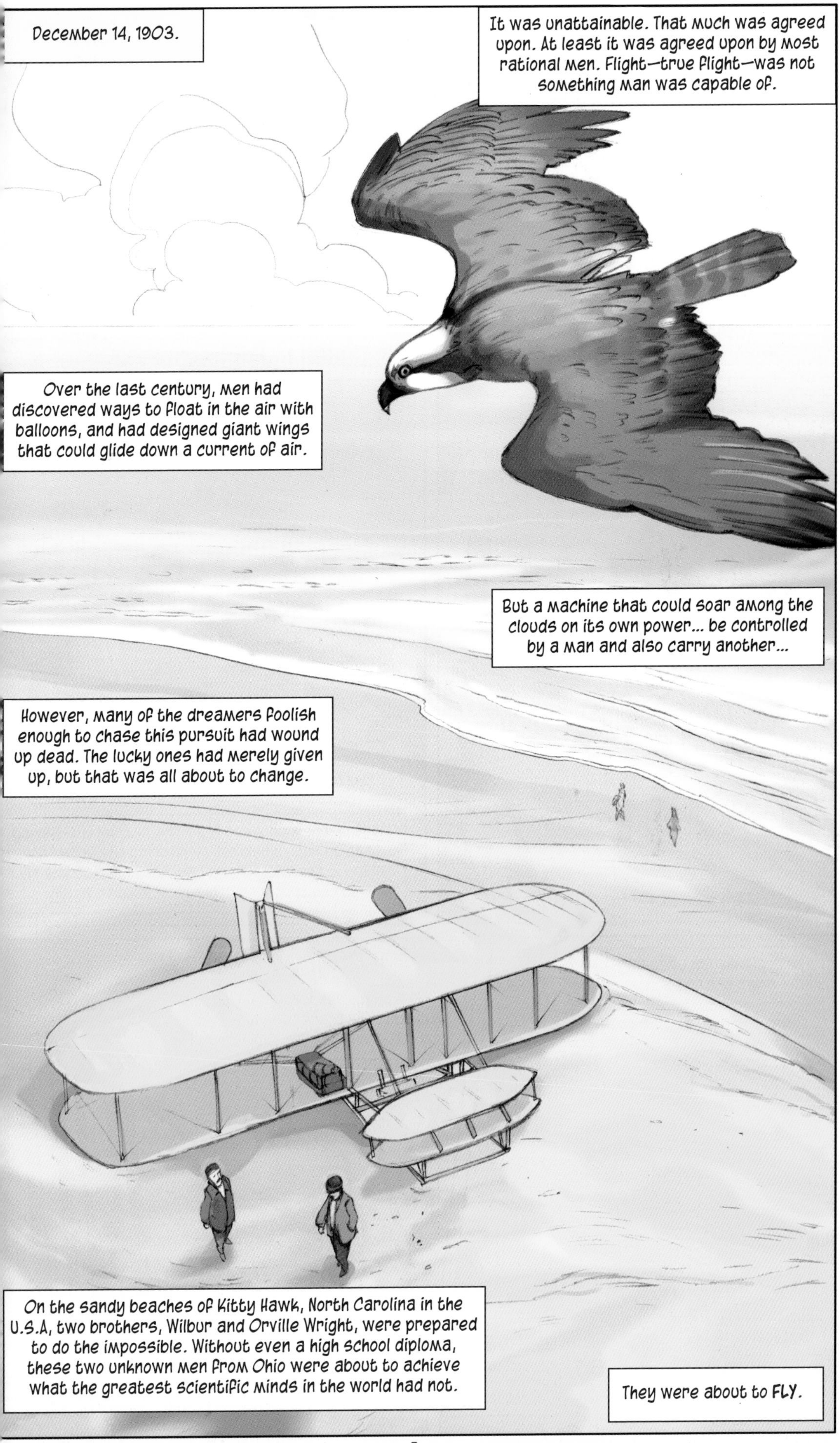
December 14, 1903.
It was unattainable. That much was agreed upon. At least it was agreed upon by most rational men. Flight—true flight—was not something man was capable of.
Over the last century, men had discovered ways to float in the air with balloons, and had designed giant wings that could glide down a current of air.
But a machine that could soar among the clouds on its own power... be controlled by a man and also carry another...
However, many of the dreamers foolish enough to chase this pursuit had wound up dead. The lucky ones had merely given up, but that was all about to change.
On the sandy beaches of Kitty Hawk, North Carolina in the U.S.A, two brothers, Wilbur and Orville Wright, were prepared to do the impossible. Without even a high school diploma, these two unknown men from Ohio were about to achieve what the greatest scientific minds in the world had not.
They were about to FLY.

This was it. They knew it. They could feel it. The moment they had been struggling toward was about to happen.

Years of research, thousands of test glides, a lifetime of dreaming, and endless hard work, had not all been in vain.

Yes, Orville. The winner gets the first chance at glory.

This coin will decide it. Right, Wilbur?

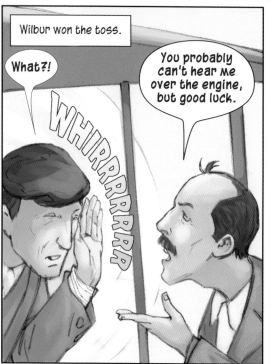

Wilbur won the toss.

What?!

You probably can't hear me over the engine, but good luck.

WHIRRRRRRR

WHIRRRRRRRR

There was an anxious crowd lined up along the beach to witness history in the making.

Most of the men were from the nearby life-saving station who, when not monitoring the ocean for ships in trouble, helped haul the glider up the hill so the brothers could glide it down again.

The craft began speeding down the track.

WHIRRRRRRRR

3 meters.

6 meters.

9 meters.

The days of failures and setbacks were over. This was it. This was the moment. The plane rose a few meters in the air and...

WHIRRRRRRR

...the engine stopped and the wing tipped to one side.

Instead of rising higher and soaring over the beach, the plane crashed back into the ground after a few seconds of flight.

KRASHH

It was not glory. It was not triumph. It was not true flight. It was...

Wilbur, are you okay?

...another delay of something the brothers had fantasized about since childhood.

Even after several setbacks, what made these two brothers still pursue their dreams?

Looks like it's just a minor damage. It shouldn't take long to repair.

Let's get to work then.

I believe it will be my turn next at the controls, Wilbur.

And what convinced them of their eventual success?

Dayton in Ohio, U.S.A. 1876.

Orville and Wilbur were named after Wilbur Fiske and Orville Dewey, two clergymen admired by their father.

The brothers probably acquired their passionate and adventurous spirit from their parents.

Now remember, Orv. You come straight home after school. Don't be late.

They got their mechanical aptitude from their mother, Susan. She had grown up helping her father in his carriage shop. Skilled with tools, she built many of their household appliances herself.

They could have got their curiosity from their father, Milton. Being a newspaper editor and an active church leader, he taught them to look for education beyond the classroom.

Captivated by technology, Orville, instead of going to school, would spend his time at his friend Ed Sines's place.

But he kept his promise to his parents...

What time is it? I promised my mother to be home in time.

One month later...

I wanted to ensure my son Orville is doing well in his studies.

Orville? Orville Wright? He hasn't been here in weeks. I assumed you took him out of this school.

The teacher's remark failed to disturb Orville's parents. They were actually relieved that he had only been stimulating his creativity.

You skipped an entire month of school?

I was at Ed's house...

They could not be angry with Orville since they encouraged their children to follow their own intellectual interests.

Aside from Orville, born on August 19, 1871, and Wilbur, who was born four years earlier on April 16, 1867...

...Milton and Susan had two older sons, Reuchlin and Lorin; and a daughter, Katharine, born three years after Orville.

Milton Wright, because of his position in church, had to move house frequently, and in 1878, they moved from Dayton to Cedar Rapids in Iowa, U.S.A.

Milton gave his kids access to his large collection of books, which had everything from classic literature to theology.

I have a surprise for you both. Do you want to see it?

He also encouraged their passionate and adventurous spirit.

He got them gifts from his travels that would expose them to a world beyond their immediate surroundings.

A world where education could even come from something as simple as...

...a toy.

A little toy made of paper, and cork, and bamboo; and powered by rubber bands that could float into the air.

And when the fragile toy broke, it was their persistence that made the boys try and make their own.

They built flying devices, each one larger and better than the previous one. These small toys were the first powered aircrafts the brothers had built together.

What are you working on, Orville? Not the lesson I assigned, I can see that much.

My brother and I plan to build a flying craft large enough to carry both of us.

But flying was not the only thing on young Orville's mind. He had a strong mischievous streak also.

And not everything he read was put to useful pursuits...

Let's form an army. Just like Napoleon. I'll be the general and you can all be the colonels and captains.

Doesn't an army need weapons?

And a mission. An army needs a mission.

A mission? Since our class was dismissed early today, let's all go back and make the other kids jealous. That will be our mission.

I just don't see the point in traveling all the way back to Richmond only for a piece of paper.

The move back to Dayton presented Wilbur with his own unique problem. He had completed his studies, and had to just go back to Richmond to receive his graduation diploma.

And as always, his family supported Wilbur's judgement.

I have received the education and that's what is important. A diploma won't change that.

As always, he discussed his options with his family.

So, what will you do next?

$A = \pi r^2$

$\left(\dfrac{6x^4 y^5 z^2}{xy^{-5} z^0}\right)^{-3}$

$\dfrac{x^2 - 4}{x + 3} \div \dfrac{x - 2}{x^2 + 5x + }$

$\int \sqrt{x^2}\, dx$

$\sqrt{25} \sqrt{x^2}$

$\sqrt[3]{8} \sqrt[n]{x}$

$\sum_{0}^{\infty} \left(\dfrac{1}{2}\right)^n$

$A(t) = A$

Wilbur harbored big plans of moving to Yale and becoming a teacher. So he enrolled in college prep classes at Dayton's Central High to improve his maths and Latin.

Excellent job, Wilbur. That's right as usual.

But life doesn't always turn out the way you plan it.

We're just down by a point. We can win this game. Wilbur, I'll pass to you as soon as--

WHAM

A freak collision while playing a game of Shinny in 1886 altered the course of Wilbur's life.

Wilbur! Wilbur, are you okay?! Somebody call a doctor.

The sharp blow battered Wilbur's face and cost him his front teeth. His injuries took a toll not only on his body but also on his mind and spirit...

Wilbur gave up on his classes at Dayton's Central High, and even his girl.

I'm heading into town, Wilbur. Do you want to come with me? We could get some ice cream. Wilbur?

He soon became depressed and reclusive. He began considering himself too frail and decided that a college degree would be a waste of time and money.

He devoted himself to caring for his mother, who had contracted tuberculosis a few years earlier.

He spent whatever time he had devouring book after book, and would rarely leave the house.

And while Wilbur was withdrawing from the outside world, Orville was throwing himself into his newest passion.

Back in Richmond, Orville had read about woodcuts, a printing technique, where a block of wood is carved, coated with ink, and the design is pressed into paper.

Orville got interested in it and Wilbur helped him create his own designs by giving him some engraving tools for Christmas.

He began using his father's letterpress to print his woodcut designs and soon developed a passion for printing.

ORVILLE WRIGHT
&
ED SINES
ALL YOUR PRINTING NEEDS

Orville was delighted to discover that his old friend Ed Sines had his own small toy printing press.

Orville's not upstairs, Father. He spends ALL his time at Ed's house with that little toy press.

If he loves it that much, I know a man who's willing to trade a real press for some timber. Do we still have that little boat we built a few years ago?

The boat leaks anyway. This was a great idea, Father.

The new and improved print shop was moved to the Wright's home. Soon, Orville and Ed started taking actual paying jobs—printing ads and flyers for local shops.

There were dozens of reasons to slow things down—Orville was still just a kid in school—but he was not one for the simple path.

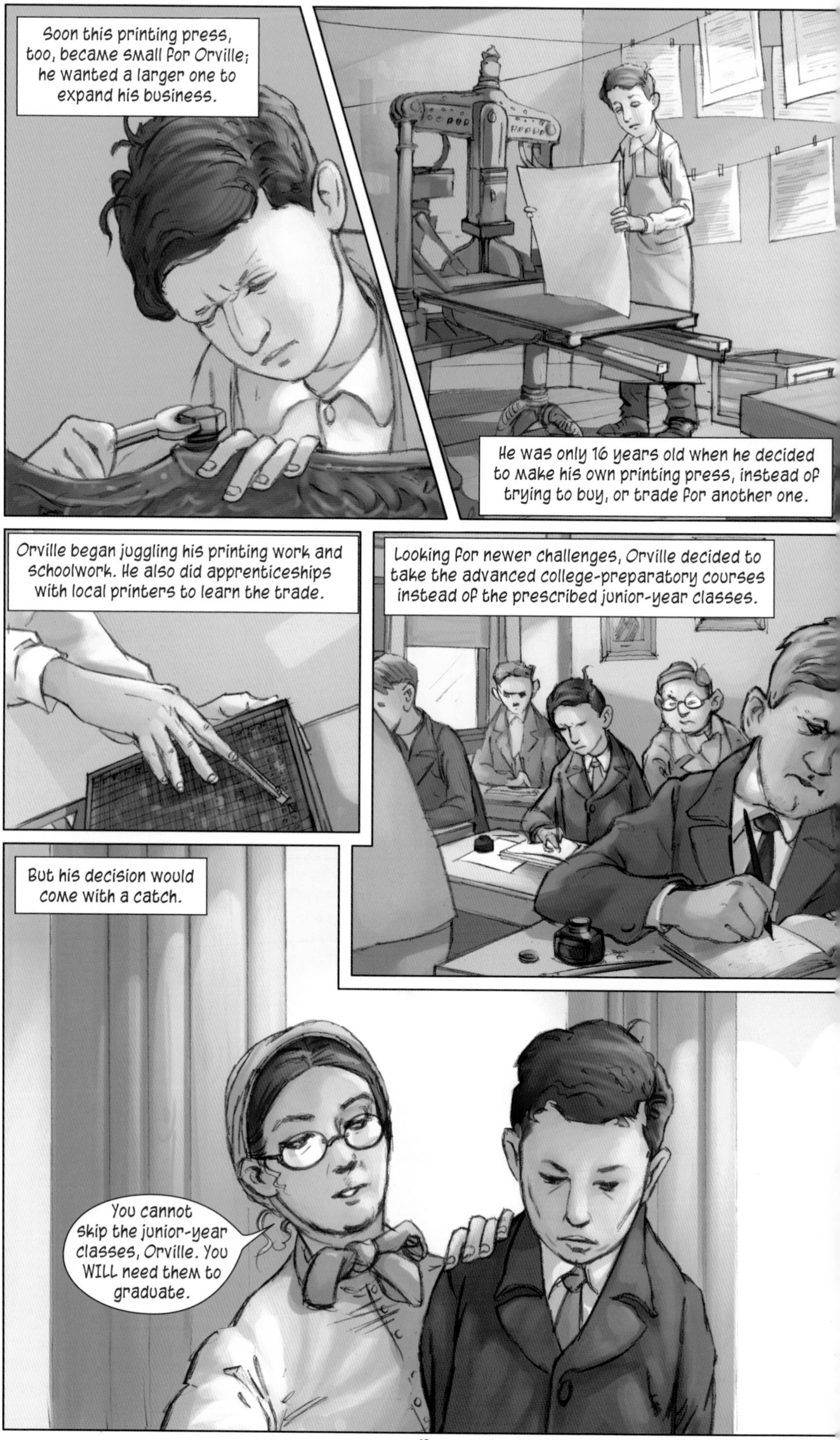
Soon this printing press, too, became small for Orville; he wanted a larger one to expand his business.
He was only 16 years old when he decided to make his own printing press, instead of trying to buy, or trade for another one.
Orville began juggling his printing work and schoolwork. He also did apprenticeships with local printers to learn the trade.
Looking for newer challenges, Orville decided to take the advanced college-preparatory courses instead of the prescribed junior-year classes.
But his decision would come with a catch.
You cannot skip the junior-year classes, Orville. You WILL need them to graduate.

But, the consequences just weren't that important to Orville. His grades had already begun to drop as he was developing interests outside of school.

Wright? Orville Wright? Is Orville here?

Or, maybe, it was the influence of his brother Wilbur, who valued actual learning over a piece of paper.

Knowing what was at stake, Orville opted to learn as much as he could and decided to skip the review courses.

And when his hard work and passion for learning were enough to qualify him for a diploma, he, too, left high school without graduating.

Orville chose to focus fulltime on his printing career. But he knew he would need help. And there was only one person he could turn to.

The person who had been by his side from day one, with whom he had shared every toy, who had helped him with every little scheme.

The person who had been his closest friend.

His brother, Wilbur.

Wilbur had devoted three years of his life to caring for his mother.

He tried to make his mother comfortable as her condition worsened, but she passed away in 1889.

Gradually, Wilbur began to come out of the depression that had plagued him for so long.

He once again started becoming the old Wilbur—passionate, articulate, intelligent, and always there to support his family.

He was already helping out his brother with building the printing press and a few print jobs.

With Milton Wright still an active church leader, Wilbur began writing essays in support of his father's views.

Orville still focussed on printing; and Wilbur, too, started taking an interest. Later, Orville bought out Ed Sines's share of the business, and gave his brother more control.

Soon the brothers found themselves in need of more space.

They rented a space in a nearby building and opened up their own print shop.

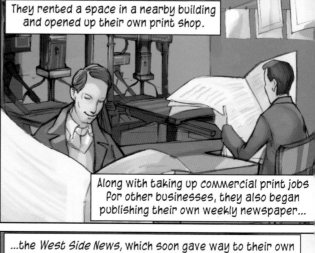

Along with taking up commercial print jobs for other businesses, they also began publishing their own weekly newspaper...

...the West Side News, which soon gave way to their own daily newspaper, covering all the local events in town.

Lilienthal's death was the turning point. This news aroused Wilbur's old childhood interest.

Have you read the news yet, Orville? It's awful.

So, Wilbur started reading every book and paper he could find on the still earthbound science of human flight.

Having injured his knee, Ed Sines was unable to work at their shop, and so they decided to sell their print shop in 1899. It was now time to start working on another interest—**flight**.

Wilbur began by contacting the Smithsonian Institution, requesting them to provide the current and crucial information on aeronautical studies.

LETTERS

They wanted to understand why the problem of flight hadn't been solved yet.

But the Smithsonian Institution was not the only place they had approached for answers. Their father had taught them to look for solutions not just from books but from the world around them.

Ok, tell me, what's your big revelation?

What if we make the wings twist like this box?

If they twist in opposite directions, it will control how the air hits the wings, and also help control the direction in which the plane moves.

You know you might be onto something.

They began by constructing a kite to test their hypothesis. Wilbur attached the two wings together with some struts and wires.

Strings connected the wings to two sticks that would allow the brothers to twist the wings from the ground.

The kite even piqued the curiosity of their nephew, Milton.

Wilbur took his creation to a local field, called Chadwick's hill, which was the favorite spot for kite flying among school children.

What's that guy doing?

The children found it strange to see a grown man flying a giant kite.

What are you doing, Mister?

I am testing my kite. If this works, I will make a flying machine.

After his trials, Wilbur was convinced that their idea was sound, and he couldn't wait to share the news with Orville...

...but he doubted the winds would be strong enough in Dayton to conduct their research.

What have you got there?

A letter from a guy called Wilbur Wright. He and his brother are doing some kind of research, and are looking for a place which has the strongest winds in the country.

Well, it doesn't get much stronger than in the windy city of Chicago.

US WEATHER BUREAU

The brothers also consulted Octave Chanute, who was a leading U.S. aviation pioneer.

He had conducted some of his own experiments in that area, and his research was among the work recommended by the Smithsonian Institute.

Dear Wilbur,

You'll find very strong winds in Chicago, but not much privacy. I would recommend San Diego in California, and St. James City in Florida as suitable locations to conduct your experiments. While these two sites have sufficient steady winds, what they lack is sand hills. And you might want to consider a place with some sand in case you experience any rough landings. I personally prefer to do the preliminary testing on a sand hill and then trying ambitious feats over water. Maybe, better locations could be also found further south.

After one last consultation with the U.S. Weather Bureau, Orville and Wilbur settled for Kitty Hawk in North Carolina, an isolated spot down south which had the sixth highest average wind speed in the country.

Food might distract me from our work, Katharine, with all the hair we have lost lately. Do you still want me to carry all this?

Jelly

Yes, I'll just put it in your suitcase. And remember to let us know once you get there. And remember to write as much as you can and...

27

Wilbur set out first to their new testing ground.

WHOOOOSH

Isn't there another boat? This doesn't exactly look--

Nothing to worry about, Mr. Wright. The storm should be passing by shortly, anyway. It should be smooth sailing.

I thought you said it would be smooth sailing!

Just keep bailing out the water. I've survived much worse and so has this ship.

SPLRAAASH

We've reached the shore. I told you there was nothing to worry about. I think I even see the sun.

September 12, 1900.

Wilbur? Wilbur Wright? We have been expecting you. As I mentioned in my letter, you will find everything you need to conduct your research here.

Thank you, Mr. Tate. Your letter certainly helped us decide on Kitty Hawk. I hope the winds live up to their reputation.

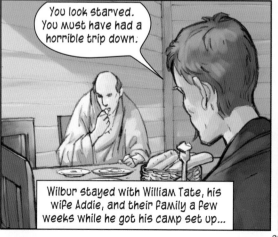

You look starved. You must have had a horrible trip down.

Wilbur stayed with William Tate, his wife Addie, and their family a few weeks while he got his camp set up...

...and Orville joined him later.

My trip down was fine, Mr. Tate. I'm sure my brother was exaggerating.

28

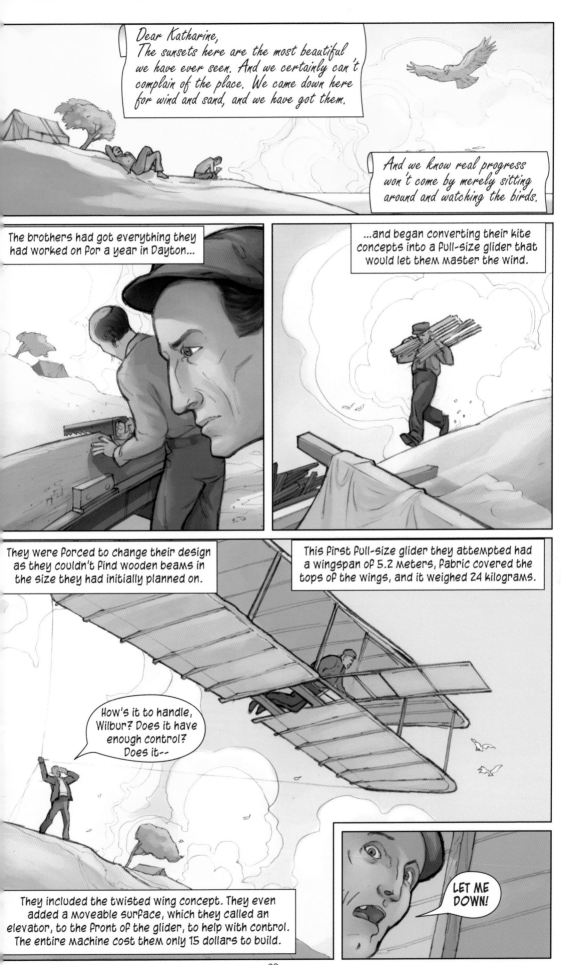

Dear Katharine,
The sunsets here are the most beautiful we have ever seen. And we certainly can't complain of the place. We came down here for wind and sand, and we have got them.

And we know real progress won't come by merely sitting around and watching the birds.

The brothers had got everything they had worked on for a year in Dayton...

...and began converting their kite concepts into a full-size glider that would let them master the wind.

They were forced to change their design as they couldn't find wooden beams in the size they had initially planned on.

This first full-size glider they attempted had a wingspan of 5.2 meters, fabric covered the tops of the wings, and it weighed 24 kilograms.

How's it to handle, Wilbur? Does it have enough control? Does it--

They included the twisted wing concept. They even added a moveable surface, which they called an elevator, to the front of the glider, to help with control. The entire machine cost them only 15 dollars to build.

LET ME DOWN!

The success that seemed to come so easily at times with their other endeavors was nowhere to be found.

It still doesn't have the type of control we want.

This wasn't like building a printing press, or a bicycle, where they could improve upon the existing designs. They were trying to build a machine that had never been built before.

Even the lift. I thought it would go up much higher.

And they had to take a step backward to advance.

In spite of all that, I actually think we are on the right track, Wilbur.

I think I agree. The wing tipped up at a different angle, but it seems like the twisting of wings is the right way.

Orville and Wilbur started by controlling their full-sized glider from the ground, like a kite.

They decided that when they had gained enough experience and knowledge of how the craft would react in the wind, they would attempt to glide again.

Their glides usually took place no more than a meter high, sometimes just centimeters, from the ground.

The goal wasn't to risk plunging 100 meters to their doom. The goal was to **gain control**.

There was one lever to move the plane up and down, and another to twist the wings and move the plane sideways.

The ideal winds they counted on for gliding, sometimes tore through camp at 96 kilometers per hour and sometimes died out altogether.

Over and over again, they pushed their glider to the top of a 30-meter high sandy dune known as Kill Devil Hills. Sometimes they attempted this on their own.

And sometimes they were aided by William Tate, or his half-brother, Daniel...

...or the men of the local life-saving station like J. T. Daniels and W. S. Dough.

After about a month of such extensive research, the brothers returned to Dayton, knowing they would revisit Kitty Hawk with an improved glider.

They left their first creation to the Tate family, to salvage what they could.

This is French satin, not something one gets in Kitty Hawk. I can make some nice dresses for our daughters with all this material.

The Wright brothers now needed to focus on their work.

They hired Charlie Taylor, an old acquaintance who had produced some parts for their bikes, to take over operations of their bike shop.

If anything comes up, tell Katharine to get in touch with us.

They returned to Kitty Hawk in 1901, choosing a new campsite a few kilometers closer to Kill Devil Hills, and received a visitor—Octave Chanute.

So, this is where you plan to break all the gliding records?

You mentioned in your letter that your new glider has a wingspan of 6.7 meters and weighs 44.5 kilograms. That's the largest glider anyone's ever attempted to fly.

While everyone pursuing the dream of flight got financial backing, the Wright brothers had decided to use their own funds.

I would like to sponsor your research.

Sorry Octave, we can't accept your generous offer to fund our research.

If you won't accept my money, at least take my help.

You need a doctor here, in case something goes wrong. I know a good man, George Spratt. He is a doctor with a keen interest in aeronautics.

No objections. And I'll even ask my associate, who is building a glider for me, to come down to help you as well...

'...his name is Edward Huffaker.'

Octave forgot to mention the mosquitoes when he said I'd love your camp.

They come and go. It helps if you bury yourself under the blankets and the netting. It doesn't make the sweltering heat any more tolerable, but it does keep the mosquitoes away.

And what happens if they bite through the netting?

I didn't think they **could** eat through the netting? **Ow! No!** There's no escape. They're chewing us clear through our underwear and socks.

Do you think we should try and warn Spratt before he gets here? Aah!

I think he's already on his way down—ow—**ow!**

A few days later, George Spratt arrived at the camp.

Why is your camp on fire?

It's just smoke. We're burning some old wood. It's the only thing that helps keep the mosquitoes away.

Cough... cough... Well, I can't breathe here. I'll take my chances with the mosquitoes.

Minutes later.

Cough... cough... The mosquitoes are worse. I'll take my chances with the smoke.

Dear Katharine,
With the weather change, the mosquitoes have finally gone away and the conditions have calmed down.

We're trying to squeeze in as much practice time with the glider as we can. Practice is the key to the secret of flying.

It has taken time, but we are finally improving on the distance we can cover— sometimes gliding more than even 90 meters.

We are still just centimeters off the ground and having difficulty getting the glider to go higher. Our lift was only a third of that predicted by the Lilienthal data, but we can't figure out where we have gone wrong, or what the real problem is. And we still need to work on the control of the machine. The elevator control has become sensitive and erratic. When we warp the wings, the glider first turns in the intended direction, and then suddenly reverses itself. We tried sealing the wings with varnish, but the problem persisted, which means the air isn't leaking through the fabric.

We are trying to not let it dampen our spirits too much. However, this season is almost over and with it, our chance to fly this year. Be back in Dayton soon. Give Dad our love.

Their spirits were dampened. Another full year gone and they still had not been able to fly. Wilbur started to think it was impossible, and even contemplated quitting.

It's not impossible, Wilbur. If you walk away from the problem it will just take that much longer to fly.

On their return to Dayton, they received a few encouraging words from Chanute, and decided to take a step backward.

They were relying on the existing data for things like air pressure, and they wanted to check them first.

These calculations had been used by pioneers like Lilienthal. But something still wasn't adding up.

Those can't be the correct numbers! Did you check them again?

You two always argue, can't you both be a bit quieter?

I checked them thrice. I know they're correct!

They wondered if the accepted data was the problem.

So they built their own wind tunnel. One by one, they tested various miniature wing shapes and discovered the most efficient wing shape.

The brothers' work was going against the earlier accepted data, but they were willing to gamble they were correct.

In just two months, they managed to analyze a tremendous amount of data.

And they were ready to head back to Kitty Hawk for a third time to test their theories.

Dear Father,
This season is shaping up to be nothing but a series of endless delays. When we reached Kitty Hawk in August, we had to first repair our camp that was ravaged in the winter storms. Thus, our new glider was delayed, and got ready only in September.

At first, we tested it like a kite and got in a few good glides, but we were delayed yet again by a bad crash. Anyway, we were not expecting things to be perfect.

If you are looking for perfect safety, you need to just sit on a fence and watch the birds. But if you really wish to learn, you must mount a machine and become acquainted with its tricks by actual trial.

We managed to finish the repairs only by the 6th of October, and since then, we are facing day after day of light winds that will not get us airborne. And the glider is so heavy, that it is a tremendous strain on everyone just to get it up back to the starting point.

October 7

October 8

October 9

October 10

At this moment, we're unsure if the conditions will improve at all.

But thankfully the conditions did pick up. This time the glider was bigger, with a wingspan of 9.8 meters and weighed 53 kilograms.

To solve the control reversal problem, they added a vertical rudder and connected it to the wing warping, thus making it easier for the pilot to manage the controls.

The theories the brothers had back in Dayton proved to be correct. Many of the control problems that had plagued them during the 1900 and 1901 seasons were gone.

One by one, they began to break all the records for gliding. They had now flown the largest glider, and held the records for the longest glide, and for gliding in the strongest winds.

They had created the world's first completely controllable glider. They logged about 1,000 glides in the fall of 1902, some traveling distances of up to 180 meters.

This 1902 glider was the first fully controlled, heavier-than-air craft, which is said to be their main invention—essentially the invention of the airplane—and more important than the 1903 biplane.

But as important as it was, this was only gliding and not flying. They were still missing a key component...

...power.

Wilbur and Orville returned to Dayton, and began contacting manufacturers to try and obtain an engine.

So the brothers decided to do it themselves.

Same as the last company we contacted. They don't have anything that would meet our specs.

With Charlie Taylor's help, they designed their own lightweight, gas-powered, four-cylinder engine.

Which means that, either they can't produce the engine we need or they won't do it.

Along with constructing their own propellers, they also had to redesign their glider to compensate for the added weight.

What if we use chains to transfer the power from the engine to the propellers? Just like the chains on a bike?

The brothers worked out a system for three-axis control that is still used today on a fixed-wing aircraft: left and right like a car or boat, up and down, and banking a turn like birds do.

It seemed like it was back to square one again when the motor broke during its first test and it had to be rebuilt again. Square one... a fourth machine...

...and a fourth trip to Kitty Hawk.

We don't need any extra money. We--

It's just a dollar for the telegram. The one to let me know the moment you've achieved success.

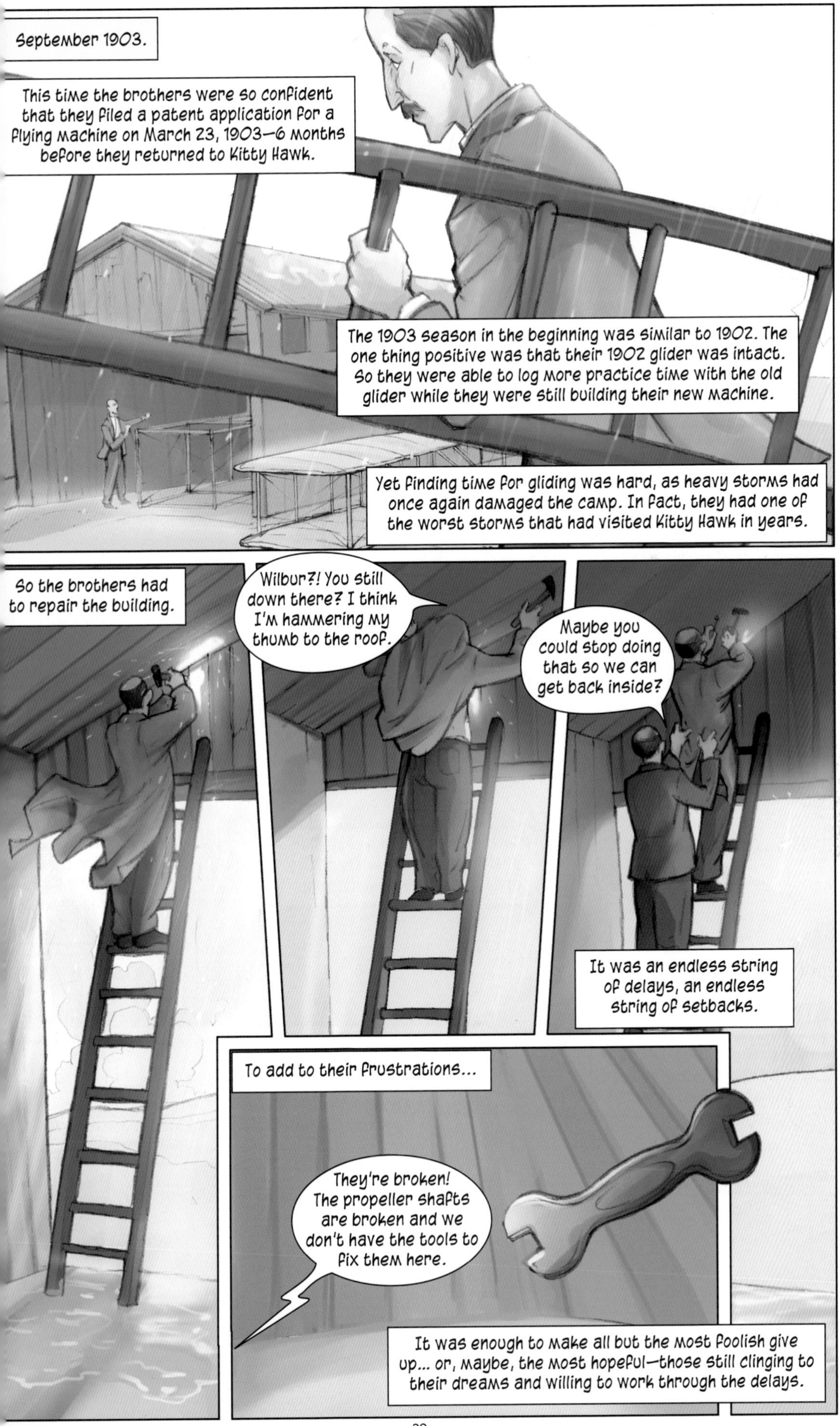
September 1903.
This time the brothers were so confident that they filed a patent application for a flying machine on March 23, 1903—6 months before they returned to Kitty Hawk.
The 1903 season in the beginning was similar to 1902. The one thing positive was that their 1902 glider was intact. So they were able to log more practice time with the old glider while they were still building their new machine.
Yet finding time for gliding was hard, as heavy storms had once again damaged the camp. In fact, they had one of the worst storms that had visited Kitty Hawk in years.
So the brothers had to repair the building.
Wilbur?! You still down there? I think I'm hammering my thumb to the roof.
Maybe you could stop doing that so we can get back inside?
It was an endless string of delays, an endless string of setbacks.
To add to their frustrations...
They're broken! The propeller shafts are broken and we don't have the tools to fix them here.
It was enough to make all but the most foolish give up... or, maybe, the most hopeful—those still clinging to their dreams and willing to work through the delays.

I guess we should send them back to Dayton. Charlie has the tools, he can fix it and ship them back to us.

And what do we do until then?

So on November 5, they sent the propeller shafts to Charlie Taylor.

The 1902 glider which had been stored indoors near a stove, had completely dried out. It was no longer safe to fly. The brothers now had nothing to practice with.

It was beginning to look like everything they had been working toward was about to slip through their fingers.

Look!

The brothers got the propeller shafts back on November 20, and set to work immediately.

Meanwhile, Samuel Langley of the Smithsonian was busy building his own plane.

If not Langley, someone else was likely to beat them.

Dear Mr. Chanute,
It is my understanding that you have seen the Wright brothers' gliders. I was hoping you could provide some detail as to the actual construction....

The letter was signed by one Mr. Glenn Curtiss.

The propeller shafts cracked again, and Orville took them back to Dayton on November 30 for repairs.

It was December and the winter winds were becoming increasingly violent. And Langley was ready to test his machine in public for a second attempt at flight.

December 8, 1903.

Yes, I am certain. My machine, which I call the Aerodrome, WILL fly this time.

Mr. Langley, are you sure that your plane will fly?

Wilbur and Orville were running out of time...

...or they would have been, if Langley's plane had actually flown. The Aerodrome crashed into water the moment it left the launching catapult.

And since that was the second time Langley's machine had failed in public, it eliminated his chance at history.

And it put the Wright brothers back in front in the race for flight.

On December 11, Orville returned to Kitty Hawk with the repaired propeller shafts.

The brothers immediately started getting their machine ready.

They decided to call this model the Wright Flyer, which now had a wingspan of over 12 meters, and weighed about 275 kilograms.

CLICK CLICK CLICK

They even constructed an 18-meter launching track and placed the Flyer on a wheeled dolly.

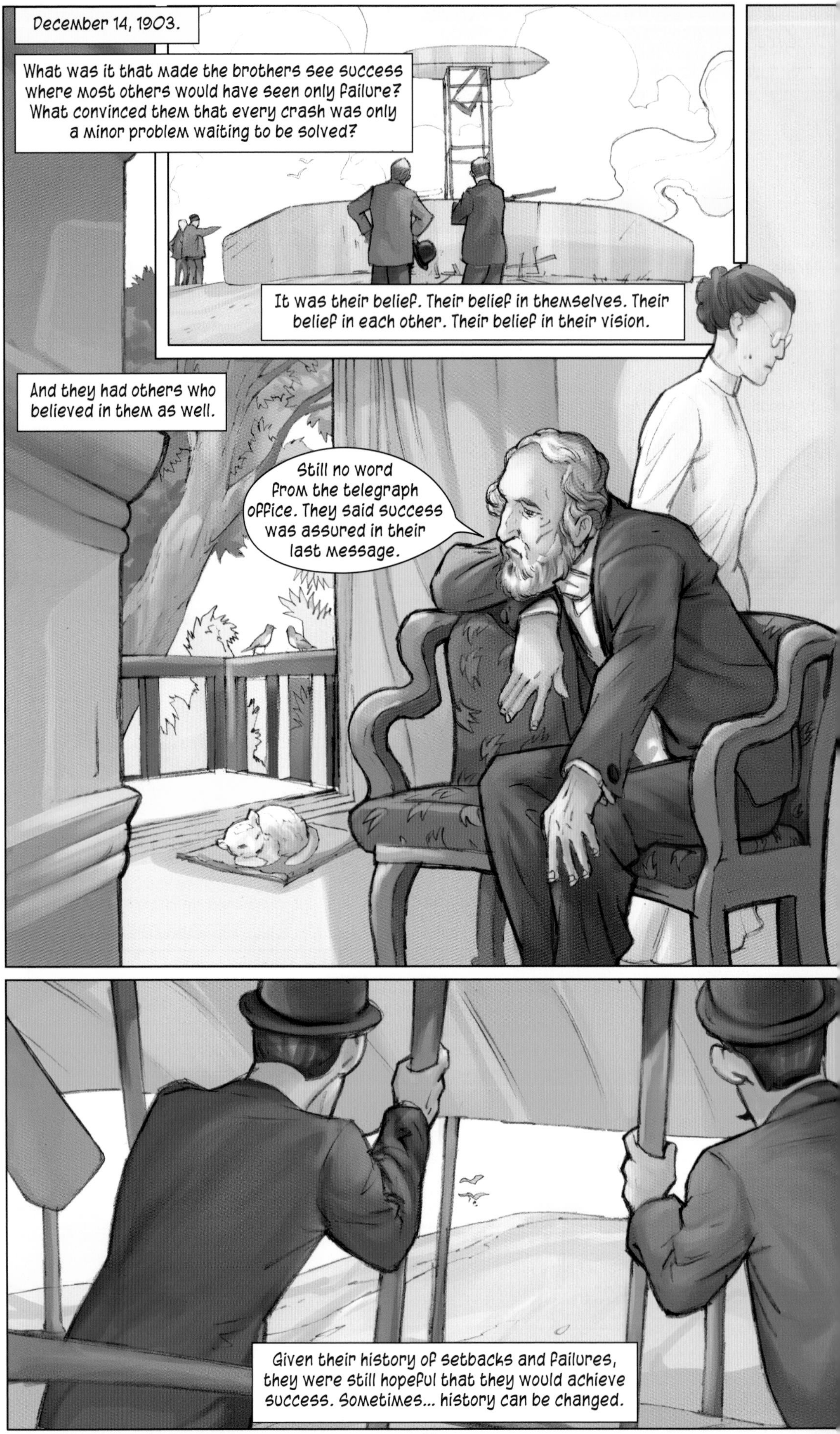
December 14, 1903.
What was it that made the brothers see success where most others would have seen only failure? What convinced them that every crash was only a minor problem waiting to be solved?
It was their belief. Their belief in themselves. Their belief in each other. Their belief in their vision.
And they had others who believed in them as well.
Still no word from the telegraph office. They said success was assured in their last message.
Given their history of setbacks and failures, they were still hopeful that they would achieve success. Sometimes... history can be changed.

December 17, 1903.

I hope those brothers wouldn't be foolish enough to attempt to fly in these rough winds.

WHOOOOSH

The weather was far from ideal. Even William Tate, who had been with them for four seasons now, didn't bother to show up.

But Wilbur and Orville were out of patience and not willing to wait any longer.

Including the railroad fares to and from Kitty Hawk, they had altogether spent almost 1,000 dollars of their own money. More importantly, they had invested years of their lives.

And what they got in return was **12 seconds**.

12 seconds! It was not a long time at all. Not enough time to do anything.

But Orville and Wilbur Wright found a way to make these 12 seconds mark history.

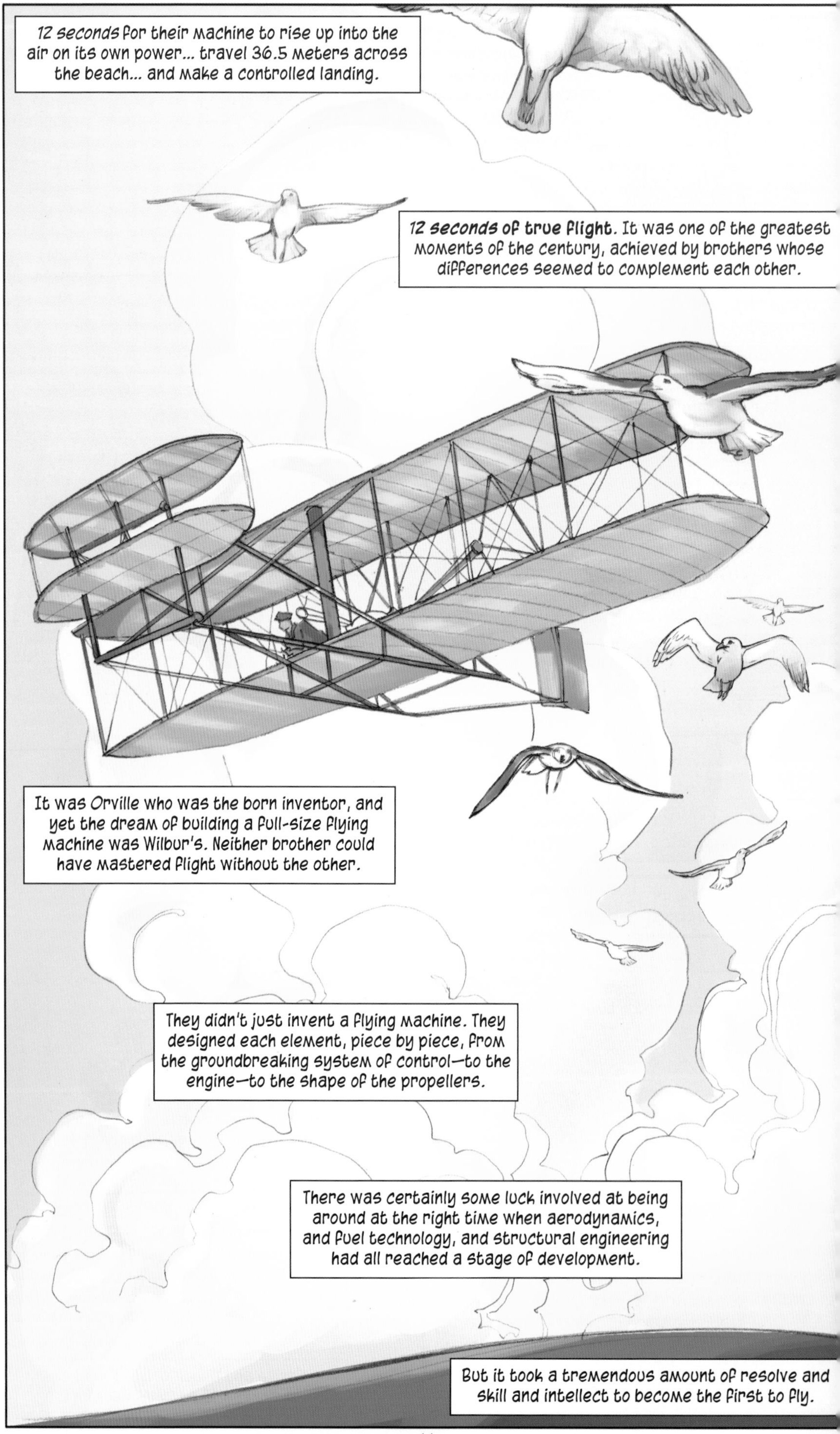

12 seconds for their machine to rise up into the air on its own power... travel 36.5 meters across the beach... and make a controlled landing.
12 seconds of true flight. It was one of the greatest moments of the century, achieved by brothers whose differences seemed to complement each other.
It was Orville who was the born inventor, and yet the dream of building a full-size flying machine was Wilbur's. Neither brother could have mastered flight without the other.
They didn't just invent a flying machine. They designed each element, piece by piece, from the groundbreaking system of control—to the engine—to the shape of the propellers.
There was certainly some luck involved at being around at the right time when aerodynamics, and fuel technology, and structural engineering had all reached a stage of development.
But it took a tremendous amount of resolve and skill and intellect to become the first to fly.

Orville and Wilbur had just achieved the impossible. But their first reaction wasn't to stop everything and alert the whole world.

Their first reaction was like that of a child testing out a new toy... they wanted to do it again.

Three more flights followed that day with the two brothers taking turns at the controls. Each flight was longer and traveled farther than the one before it.

The fourth flight lasted just under a minute and traveled about 260 meters.

And it soon proved to be the final flight of the season.

Extraordinary. I'm not sure any of us would have believed it if we hadn't been here watching it. What did it feel like to be up there?

The wind's too strong. We can't hold it. Everyone let go. Let go J. T.!

It felt like—oh no! The Flyer!

Heellllp!

The strong winter winds that had so severely limited their practice time took hold of the plane.

And in about the same amount of time that it took for the brothers to make history...

...their machine was damaged too much and was rendered irreparable for them to try again.

Are you all right? It's miraculous you weren't killed.

I'll be fine. I don't think anything's broken. Not my bones at least.

As unfortunate as that incident was, it could not erase what Orville and Wilbur managed to achieve.

Nor was it enough to dampen their spirits or prevent them from trekking 6.5 kilometers to the local telegram station to notify their father and sister about their success.

FLIGHT! On a beach in Kitty Hawk? Is this for real?!

The telegraph operator at the Norfolk office wants to know if they can transmit your news to the papers, Mr. Wright.

Tell him **only** to our father. We do not want to go public yet.

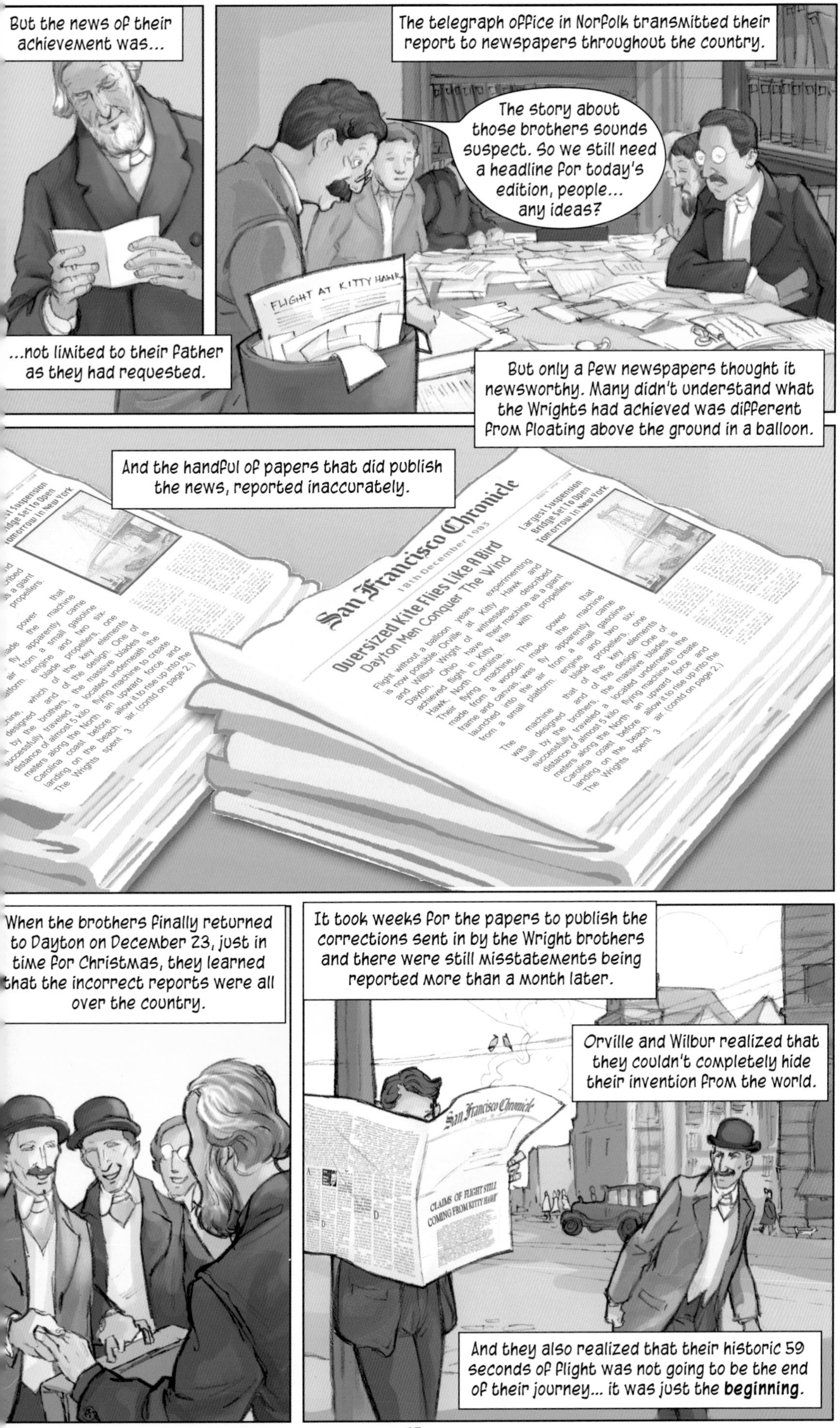
But the news of their achievement was...
...not limited to their father as they had requested.
The telegraph office in Norfolk transmitted their report to newspapers throughout the country.
FLIGHT AT KITTY HAWK
The story about those brothers sounds suspect. So we still need a headline for today's edition, people... any ideas?
But only a few newspapers thought it newsworthy. Many didn't understand what the Wrights had achieved was different from floating above the ground in a balloon.
And the handful of papers that did publish the news, reported inaccurately.
San Francisco Chronicle
Oversized Kite Flies Like A Bird
Dayton Men Conquer The Wind
Largest Suspension Bridge Set To Open Tomorrow In New York
When the brothers finally returned to Dayton on December 23, just in time for Christmas, they learned that the incorrect reports were all over the country.
It took weeks for the papers to publish the corrections sent in by the Wright brothers and there were still misstatements being reported more than a month later.
San Francisco Chronicle
CLAIMS OF FLIGHT STILL COMING FROM KITTY HAWK
Orville and Wilbur realized that they couldn't completely hide their invention from the world.
And they also realized that their historic 59 seconds of flight was not going to be the end of their journey... it was just the **beginning**.

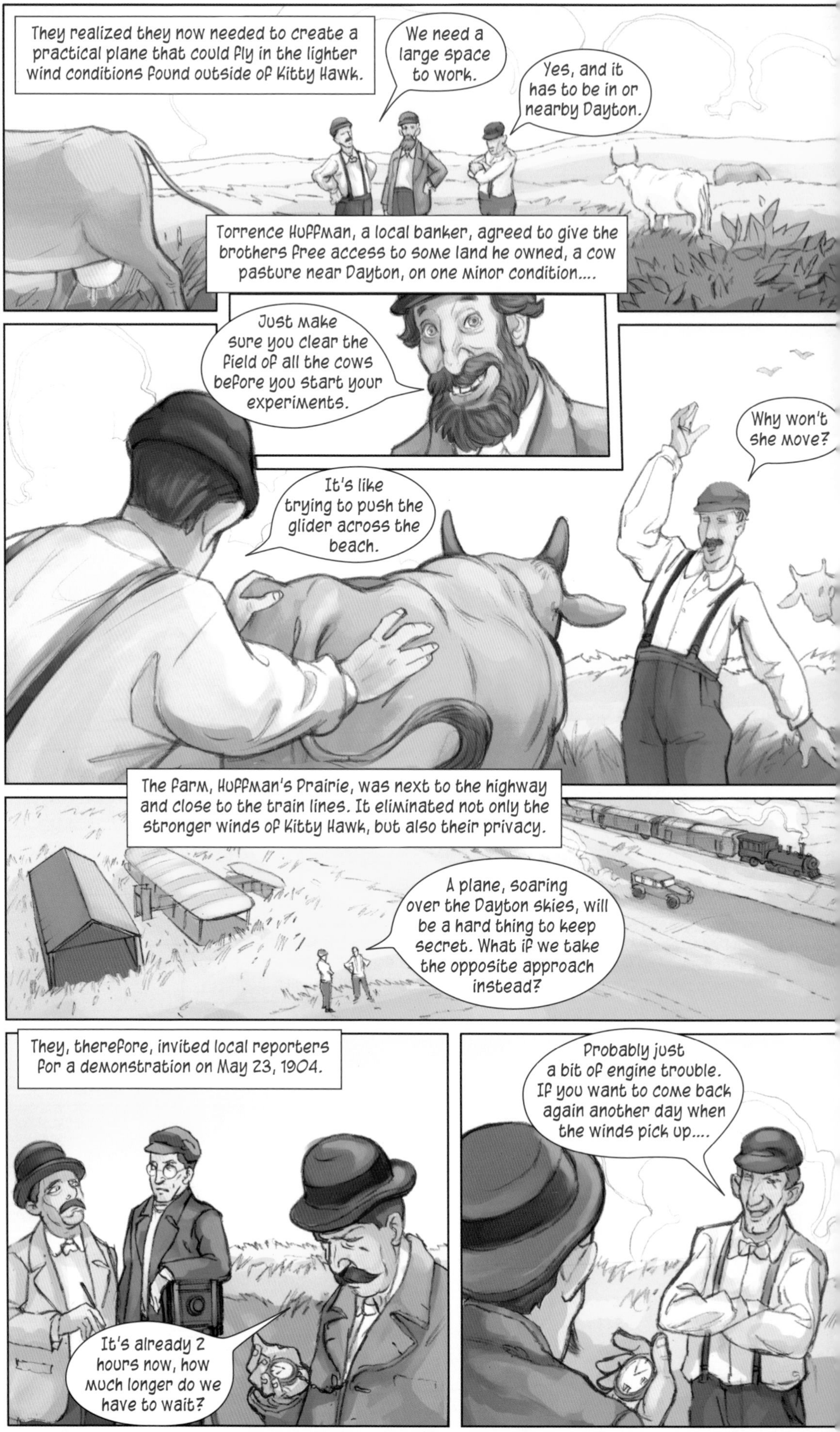

They realized they now needed to create a practical plane that could fly in the lighter wind conditions found outside of Kitty Hawk.
We need a large space to work.
Yes, and it has to be in or nearby Dayton.
Torrence Huffman, a local banker, agreed to give the brothers free access to some land he owned, a cow pasture near Dayton, on one minor condition....
Just make sure you clear the field of all the cows before you start your experiments.
It's like trying to push the glider across the beach.
Why won't she move?
The farm, Huffman's Prairie, was next to the highway and close to the train lines. It eliminated not only the stronger winds of Kitty Hawk, but also their privacy.
A plane, soaring over the Dayton skies, will be a hard thing to keep secret. What if we take the opposite approach instead?
They, therefore, invited local reporters for a demonstration on May 23, 1904.
It's already 2 hours now, how much longer do we have to wait?
Probably just a bit of engine trouble. If you want to come back again another day when the winds pick up....

A handful of reporters did return a few days later and witnessed another engine malfunction.

From then on, the brothers were left alone to do their work in private, which they did.

And on September 20, they completed their first circular flight, traveling 1.24 kilometers in 1 minute and 36 seconds.

This meant they could now turn their plane in the direction they wanted.

Do you think the government would be interested in our invention?

We could contact our congressman, Robert Nevin. We could offer to develop a plane for the military.

A few weeks later.

It looks like a form letter. I doubt that congressman Nevin vouching for us made any difference.

And thus they started focussing on the business aspect of the invention.

They did not understand the extent of what the Wright brothers had already achieved. The army had earlier invested in Langley's aircraft, and did not want to repeat their mistake.

On October 5, 1905, Wilbur circled a field 30 times, a distance of 39.4 kilometers, and remained in the air for over 39 minutes.

This new plane was the world's **first** practical airplane. It could fly figure eights with ease and turn. But it was all done privately and without witnesses—so the world still had **no clue**.

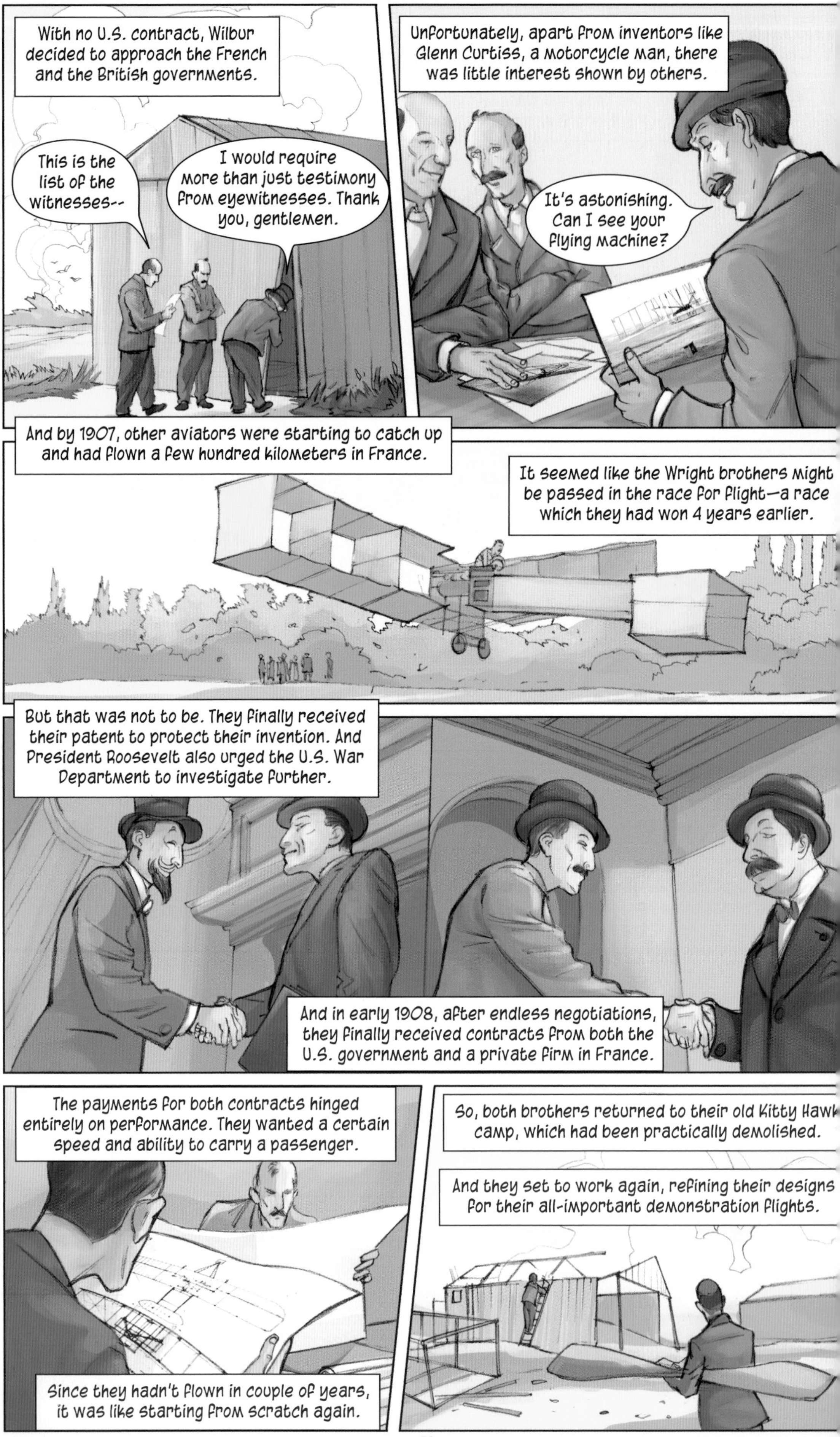

With no U.S. contract, Wilbur decided to approach the French and the British governments.
This is the list of the witnesses--
I would require more than just testimony from eyewitnesses. Thank you, gentlemen.
Unfortunately, apart from inventors like Glenn Curtiss, a motorcycle man, there was little interest shown by others.
It's astonishing. Can I see your flying machine?
And by 1907, other aviators were starting to catch up and had flown a few hundred kilometers in France.
It seemed like the Wright brothers might be passed in the race for flight—a race which they had won 4 years earlier.
But that was not to be. They finally received their patent to protect their invention. And President Roosevelt also urged the U.S. War Department to investigate further.
And in early 1908, after endless negotiations, they finally received contracts from both the U.S. government and a private firm in France.
The payments for both contracts hinged entirely on performance. They wanted a certain speed and ability to carry a passenger.
Since they hadn't flown in couple of years, it was like starting from scratch again.
So, both brothers returned to their old Kitty Hawk camp, which had been practically demolished.
And they set to work again, refining their designs for their all-important demonstration flights.

Leaving his brother to focus on the U.S. contract, Wilbur then traveled to Europe on May 17, 1908, reaching France 11 days later.

He spent months just repairing the plane, which had been damaged during shipping. It was a redesigned model, which now allowed the pilot to sit upright instead of lying on his stomach.

And on August 8, he was ready for his first public flight.

The crowd expected Wilbur to fail. They couldn't imagine anyone could have progressed farther than their French aviators Henri Farman or Leon Delagrange.

Farman was said to be the first to fly in Europe. It didn't matter to them that Orville and Wilbur had flown years before Farman had even left the ground.

The crowd did expect to witness something special. They could feel it. And they were right.

What happened next was not special...

It was **spectacular**.

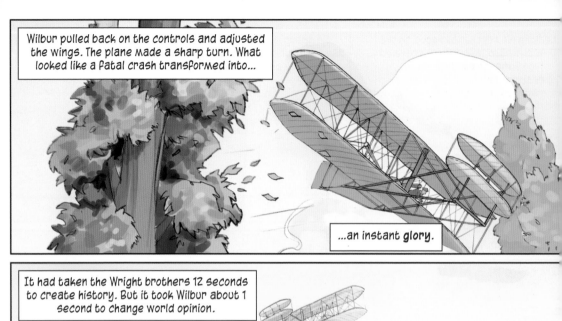

Wilbur pulled back on the controls and adjusted the wings. The plane made a sharp turn. What looked like a fatal crash transformed into...

...an instant **glory**.

It had taken the Wright brothers 12 seconds to create history. But it took Wilbur about 1 second to change world opinion.

That sharp turn that avoided a disaster proved just how superior their machine was to their competitors. No one had ever demonstrated this kind of control before.

In just *2 laps* around the airfield, Wilbur proved it wasn't just a pipedream. In just *2 laps*, Wilbur silenced all the critics.

In just *2 laps*, Wilbur became a **world hero** and a celebrity and an overnight sensation.

The public clamored for news about Wilbur.

The whole country was fascinated, obsessing over everything from his education to his family life to his social life...

...or his lack of a social life.

Who's he seeing? He must be seeing someone. I wonder if she's from America. Or do you think he has a girl here in Paris?

I hear that he hasn't seen anyone since he's been in France. He's not even staying in an apartment.

'He lives in his hangar. He sleeps there, working day and night. His only company is a stray dog that wandered in one day. He calls him *Flyer*.'

Wilbur didn't have a moment of privacy. Fans followed him everywhere. It was a totally different experience than toiling away on the secluded beaches of North Carolina.

He was indifferent to the attention and sometimes even annoyed by the crowds. But it was all part of his historic achievement.

This life of fame wasn't a life that Wilbur craved for.

Wilbur had done his part. He had conquered Europe. And now it was Orville's turn to conquer America.

While Wilbur took his plane to France, Orville remained in the U.S. to finish up a new model for the contract with the U.S. Army.

He traveled to Fort Myer, Virginia in August to prepare this model and began the test flights in September.

A crowd of thousands watched in awe as Orville flew in the air for more than an hour. He set 9 world records in a matter of days.

But Orville wasn't there to dazzle a crowd, he was trying to meet the requirements laid out by the U.S. Army—requirement to be able to fly with a passenger.

So on September 17, 1908, Lieutenant Thomas Selfridge volunteered to accompany Orville into the skies.

WIRRRRRRRRRRR

WIRRRRR TUNGGG

The Flyer went up without a problem and flew 3 laps around the parade ground at an altitude of approximately 45 meters.

What neither man knew was that one of the new propeller blades, that had been installed minutes before the flight, had a crack.

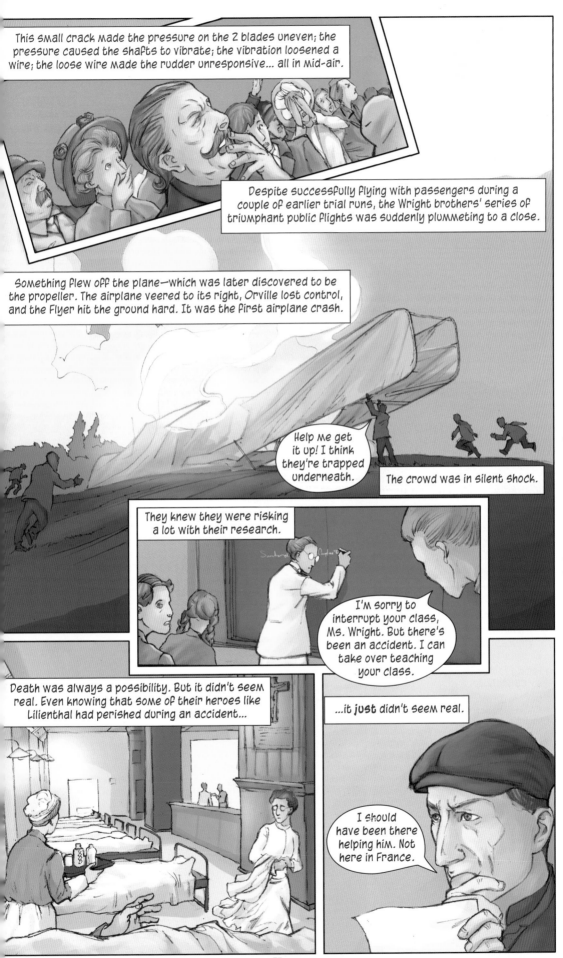

This small crack made the pressure on the 2 blades uneven; the pressure caused the shafts to vibrate; the vibration loosened a wire; the loose wire made the rudder unresponsive... all in mid-air.

Despite successfully flying with passengers during a couple of earlier trial runs, the Wright brothers' series of triumphant public flights was suddenly plummeting to a close.

Something flew off the plane—which was later discovered to be the propeller. The airplane veered to its right, Orville lost control, and the Flyer hit the ground hard. It was the first airplane crash.

Help me get it up! I think they're trapped underneath.

The crowd was in silent shock.

They knew they were risking a lot with their research.

I'm sorry to interrupt your class, Ms. Wright. But there's been an accident. I can take over teaching your class.

Death was always a possibility. But it didn't seem real. Even knowing that some of their heroes like Lilienthal had perished during an accident...

...it just didn't seem real.

I should have been there helping him. Not here in France.

Death was real now. But it was not Orville who paid the price.

Lieutenant Selfridge, Orville's passenger, was killed during the crash. And Orville was injured and spent the next couple of months recuperating in the Army hospital.

I'll stay by your side until you get well.

Although the extent of his injuries went unnoticed at the time, it would later lead to sufferings from fractures in his hip.

Wilbur was relieved to know that not only would Orville recover soon, but also that it was just a cracked propeller that caused the crash.

With Orville temporarily out of commission, the job of proving how much more their planes could achieve fell solely on Wilbur's shoulders.

Camp d'Auvours, France. September 21, 1908.

See that, Flyer. He's going to be okay!

He broke the existing records by traveling 66 kilometers in just over 90 minutes.

And he receives 1,000 dollars from The Aero Club de France.

October 10, 1908.

1 hour and 10 minutes! It's a new world record for a flight with a passenger.

Wilbur collected another 1,000 francs for setting a new altitude record of 90 meters—a record that lasted all of 5 days... until Wilbur broke it again.

By December 31, 1908, Wilbur had remained airborne for 2 hours and 20 minutes while flying 145 kilometers. It was yet another world record for flight time.

And once Orville recovered, he and Katharine joined Wilbur in Europe in January 1909...

...and got a taste of the adulation that Wilbur had been experiencing.

It's them! It's Orville and Wilbur Wright!

The brothers met kings and world leaders. They traveled through Europe demonstrating their invention and training pilots.

Merely having a chance to set the weight that would launch the plane into the air was considered an honor; one relished by even prime ministers and ambassadors.

Triumphant overseas, both brothers finally returned home to a hero's welcome.

It is my pleasure today to award the Congressional Medal of Honor to Dayton's very own Orville and Wilbur Wright.

I guess it was a good thing they decided to focus on more than just printing and bicycles.

They were joined by their family, dear old friends like Ed Sines and many others.

The brothers continued to receive numerous prizes and medals, including the Legion of Honor in June 1909.

With the French contract squared away, the brothers still had to finalize their U.S. contract.

They had to prove their plane could fly cross-country with a passenger, and land undamaged.

So in July 1909, Orville was charged with flying to a point 8 kilometers away, and returning to where he began.

I don't see him.

Maybe he got lost or maybe--

There was no maybe. The plane flew 16 kilometers in 14 minutes at a speed of about 69 kilometers per hour.

The army contract was made. Orville and Wilbur would be paid 30,000 dollars for their plane.

WIRRRRRRRRRR...

It seemed there was nothing their planes couldn't do.

On September 29, 1909, Wilbur circled the Statue of Liberty with a canoe strapped to the plane—just in case he needed to land in the water.

There wasn't any need for a water landing. And few days later on October 4, 1909, Wilbur flew for his largest audience, soaring up the Hudson River.

This marvelous invention, that had been a secret just a few years earlier, was now being witnessed by millions.

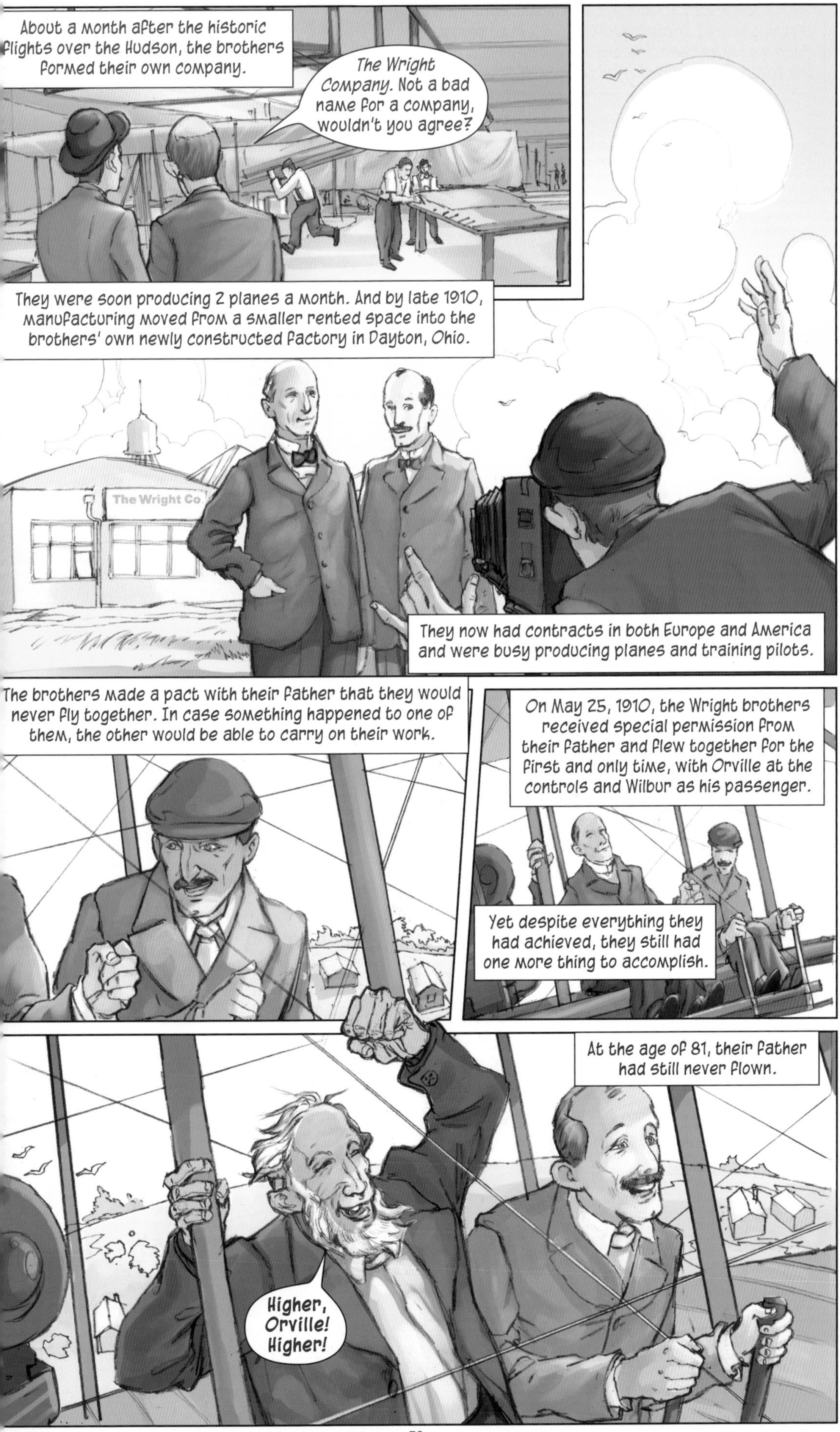

About a month after the historic flights over the Hudson, the brothers formed their own company.
The Wright Company. Not a bad name for a company, wouldn't you agree?
They were soon producing 2 planes a month. And by late 1910, manufacturing moved from a smaller rented space into the brothers' own newly constructed factory in Dayton, Ohio.
The Wright Co.
They now had contracts in both Europe and America and were busy producing planes and training pilots.
The brothers made a pact with their father that they would never fly together. In case something happened to one of them, the other would be able to carry on their work.
On May 25, 1910, the Wright brothers received special permission from their father and flew together for the first and only time, with Orville at the controls and Wilbur as his passenger.
Yet despite everything they had achieved, they still had one more thing to accomplish.
At the age of 81, their father had still never flown.
Higher, Orville! Higher!

Nothing left to accomplish. Nothing left to prove. That may have been how the Wright brothers saw the world. But it wasn't how the world saw things.

The Wright brothers were the **kings** of the sky. And everyone else was looking to claim the throne. **Everyone** else had something to prove.

Aviators began training teams of flyers for air traveling, also for doing increasingly dangerous stunts. Reluctantly, Orville and Wilbur were forced to keep up.

Orville focussed on supervising production at their factory and Wilbur focused on protecting their invention in court—preventing rival aviators from stealing their designs.

Wilbur and Orville started by funding their own experiments with their extra cash. What they intended to create was a flying machine. What they hadn't intended on was creating a new industry where anyone with a plane stood to earn significant money.

Rival companies were constantly popping up, with the majority of them simply copying the brothers' designs. Many went so far as to claim some of the Wrights' breakthroughs as their own discoveries.

They too began training pilots and put together their own team of flyers and started battling rival companies in court to protect their invention.

What began as a hobby was now a business. What began as a passion was turning into nothing but an endless stream of paperwork.

With rival companies stealing their designs, Wilbur chose to fight for their rights. It was a matter of principle.

Your Honor, we received a patent in 1906 for our designs and for the wing-warping technology we invented. As per our patent, we should be getting 10 percent as royalty on every plane sold.

The most intense of these court battles was against a rival aviator, Glenn Curtiss, who had visited the brothers back in 1906.

By 1908, Curtiss, the organization's director of experiments, used the information to build his own plane.

A couple years later after his visit, the brothers had received a request from the Aerial Experiment Association.

The group, formed by telephone inventor Alexander Graham Bell, wanted some advice on constructing a glider. Respecting Bell, and believing an organization attached to him would not violate their patent, the brothers had forwarded the information.

Orville wrote to remind Curtiss of their patent and was assured he will not be exhibiting any planes.

But a year later, Curtiss formed his own company to build and exhibit planes based on the Wright brothers' designs.

January 1910.

The courts recognized that the ailerons were based on Wright's concept of wing warping.

I rule in favor of Wilbur Wright.

It's totally different. Instead of the entire wing twisting like on the Wright's planes, I just have a small flap that tilts up or down, which I call an aileron.

February 1910.

Despite the court order, Curtiss kept searching for loopholes to keep producing his planes without paying royalty to the Wright Brothers.

I rule in favor of Wilbur Wright. Mr. Curtiss, you must stop producing your planes.

Wilbur was spending all of his time battling men like Glenn Curtiss in court. What he yearned for was a chance to return to the skies and invent again.

But he never got that chance. On May 30, 1912, Wilbur Wright passed away.

WRIGHT

Wilbur had been diagnosed with malaria, but later the doctors blamed his death on typhoid.

It was the stress of the court battles. I know it! I will now finish what Wilbur started.

January 1914.

Next time we should use a different argument. My aileron design has a separate control for each wing, while Wrights' patent specifies that the controls for the wings are connected.

It was an endless string of court battles.

With Wilbur gone, Orville was now bogged down in paperwork, and had no time left to refine their planes or to improve their designs.

The Wright brothers' planes were now being surpassed by the competition. And Orville decided to move on.

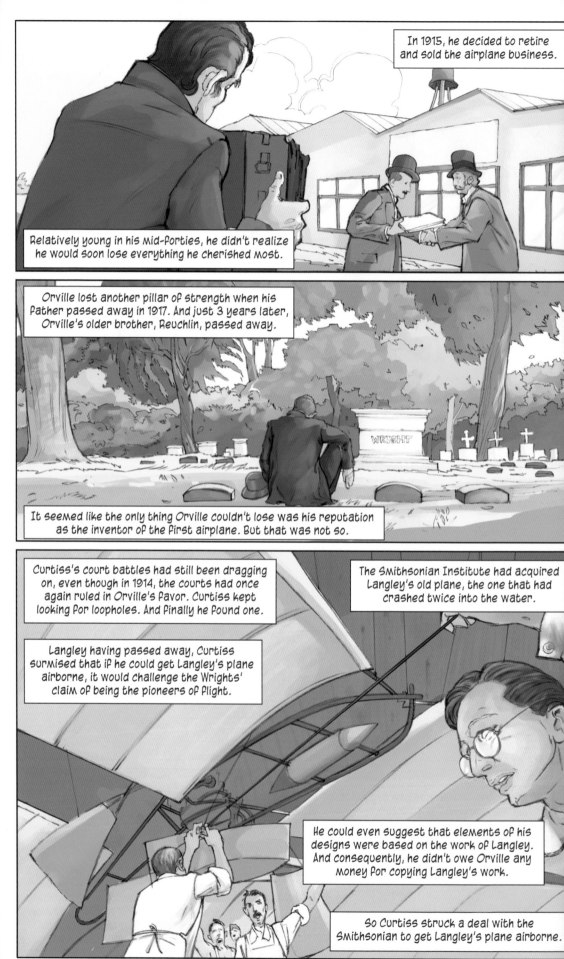

In 1915, he decided to retire and sold the airplane business.

Relatively young in his mid-forties, he didn't realize he would soon lose everything he cherished most.

Orville lost another pillar of strength when his father passed away in 1917. And just 3 years later, Orville's older brother, Reuchlin, passed away.

It seemed like the only thing Orville couldn't lose was his reputation as the inventor of the first airplane. But that was not so.

Curtiss's court battles had still been dragging on, even though in 1914, the courts had once again ruled in Orville's favor. Curtiss kept looking for loopholes. And finally he found one.

Langley having passed away, Curtiss surmised that if he could get Langley's plane airborne, it would challenge the Wrights' claim of being the pioneers of flight.

The Smithsonian Institute had acquired Langley's old plane, the one that had crashed twice into the water.

He could even suggest that elements of his designs were based on the work of Langley. And consequently, he didn't owe Orville any money for copying Langley's work.

So Curtiss struck a deal with the Smithsonian to get Langley's plane airborne.

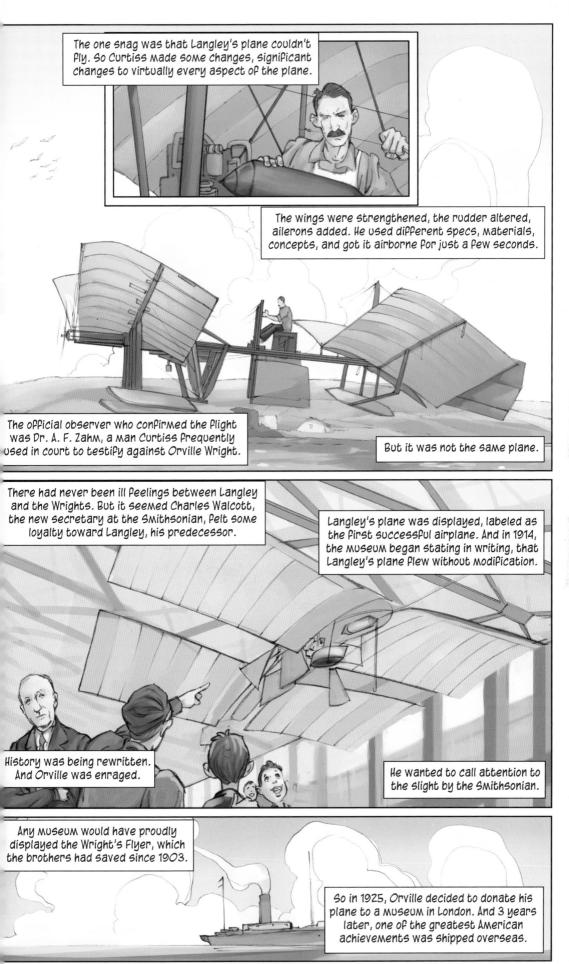

The one snag was that Langley's plane couldn't fly. So Curtiss made some changes, significant changes to virtually every aspect of the plane.

The wings were strengthened, the rudder altered, ailerons added. He used different specs, materials, concepts, and got it airborne for just a few seconds.

The official observer who confirmed the flight was Dr. A. F. Zahm, a man Curtiss frequently used in court to testify against Orville Wright.

But it was not the same plane.

There had never been ill feelings between Langley and the Wrights. But it seemed Charles Walcott, the new secretary at the Smithsonian, felt some loyalty toward Langley, his predecessor.

Langley's plane was displayed, labeled as the first successful airplane. And in 1914, the museum began stating in writing, that Langley's plane flew without modification.

History was being rewritten. And Orville was enraged.

He wanted to call attention to the slight by the Smithsonian.

Any museum would have proudly displayed the Wright's Flyer, which the brothers had saved since 1903.

So in 1925, Orville decided to donate his plane to a museum in London. And 3 years later, one of the greatest American achievements was shipped overseas.

Throughout Katharine had continued to live with her brothers and father.

But now with Orville retired, Katharine decided to move on. So in 1926, she got married and moved to Kansas City.

Orville felt abandoned for he was dependent on Katharine.

Orville was now living in a new home in Oakwood, Ohio since 1914, which he and Wilbur had designed together.

In the midst of all this, the rest of the world still viewed him as a pioneer and a hero.

Katharine's marriage created a rift in their close relationship until just before her death in 1929.

On April 8, 1930, Orville was awarded the very first *Daniel Guggenheim Medal* for great achievements in aeronautics.

Orville also built his own aeronautics laboratory and even served as a consulting engineer on the first guided missile during World War I.

He remained a public figure in the world of aviation, serving as a member of the National Advisory Committee on Aeronautics for 28 years. This organization was renamed NASA in 1958.

In 1932, Orville returned to Kitty Hawk for the dedication of a national monument to honor their achievements.

By 1939, Orville's last sibling, his brother Lorin, died.

But in typical Wright fashion, Orville kept pushing—for one last thing.

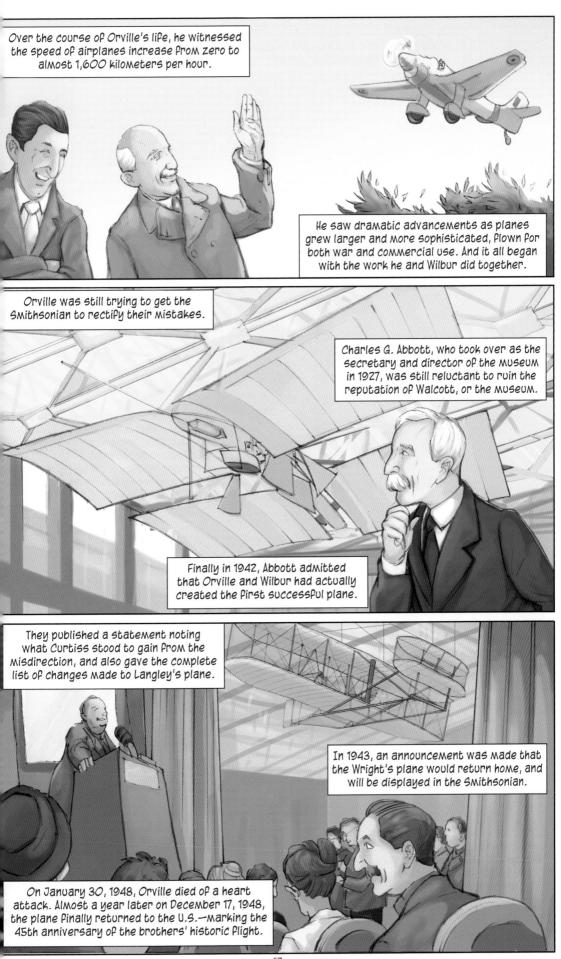

Over the course of Orville's life, he witnessed the speed of airplanes increase from zero to almost 1,600 kilometers per hour.

He saw dramatic advancements as planes grew larger and more sophisticated, flown for both war and commercial use. And it all began with the work he and Wilbur did together.

Orville was still trying to get the Smithsonian to rectify their mistakes.

Charles G. Abbott, who took over as the secretary and director of the museum in 1927, was still reluctant to ruin the reputation of Walcott, or the museum.

Finally in 1942, Abbott admitted that Orville and Wilbur had actually created the first successful plane.

They published a statement noting what Curtiss stood to gain from the misdirection, and also gave the complete list of changes made to Langley's plane.

In 1943, an announcement was made that the Wright's plane would return home, and will be displayed in the Smithsonian.

On January 30, 1948, Orville died of a heart attack. Almost a year later on December 17, 1948, the plane finally returned to the U.S.—marking the 45th anniversary of the brothers' historic flight.

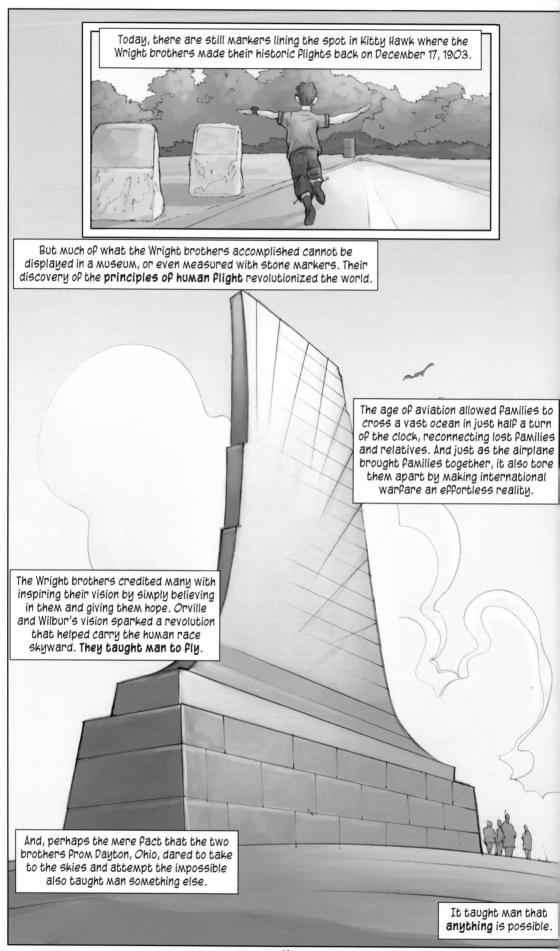

Today, there are still markers lining the spot in Kitty Hawk where the Wright brothers made their historic flights back on December 17, 1903.

But much of what the Wright brothers accomplished cannot be displayed in a museum, or even measured with stone markers. Their discovery of the **principles of human flight** revolutionized the world.

The age of aviation allowed families to cross a vast ocean in just half a turn of the clock, reconnecting lost families and relatives. And just as the airplane brought families together, it also tore them apart by making international warfare an effortless reality.

The Wright brothers credited many with inspiring their vision by simply believing in them and giving them hope. Orville and Wilbur's vision sparked a revolution that helped carry the human race skyward. **They taught man to fly.**

And, perhaps the mere fact that the two brothers from Dayton, Ohio, dared to take to the skies and attempt the impossible also taught man something else.

It taught man that **anything** is possible.

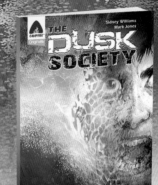

Sidney Williams
Mark Jones

THE DUSK SOCIETY

ILLUSTRATED BY NARESH KUMAR

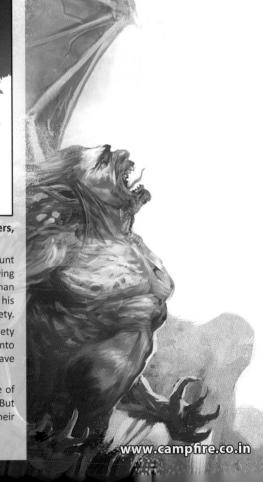

A secret society created to save the world, terrifying monsters, and magical weapons come to life in this spine-chilling tale.

Pembleton was the most boring place in the world until Count Dracula, Doctor Frankenstein, and a whole host of terrifying monsters moved in. They are under the leadership of an evil man known as Pierceblood. The only thing stopping Pierceblood, and his creatures of darkness, from destroying the world is The Dusk Society.

A secret organization created after World War I, The Dusk Society was formed to ensure that ancient, magical weapons do not fall into the wrong hands. Pierceblood is their greatest enemy, and they have waged a secret war against him for decades.

Now the conflict has come to small town America, and the fate of the world lies in the hands of The Dusk Society's newest recruits. But will they be able to overcome their differences and combine their newly discovered talents to stop Pierceblood's evil plan?

The final battle will take place on Halloween.

TAKING TO THE SKIES

How did we learn to fly? Right from the time of Leonardo da Vinci's sketch of the *Flying Machine*, centuries of research have gone into trying to fly. A master artist and inventor, da Vinci's *Flying Machine*, unfortunately remained just a sketch on paper. Despite many efforts by many people, the machine failed to fly and proved that his idea was impractical.

The first person to build and fly gliders was the German engineer Otto Lilienthal. He made hundreds of flights, starting in 1891. Lilienthal launched himself from hills hanging under his gliders. Unlike the Wright Brothers, he was unable to design a controlled and powered flight. Unfortunately, he died when his glider crashed in 1896.

The dream of flying finally came true when the Wright Brothers launched the world's first powered lighter than air machine. Though it was nothing more than a 'hop', it changed the world forever and marked the beginning of the age of the airplane.

> 'If birds can glide for long periods of time, then... why can't I?'
>
> —Orville Wright

The Wright Brothers charged $25,000 for *Miss Columbia*, the first airplane purchased by the American Government; but a bonus of $5,000 was awarded because the plane's speed exceeded the specified maximum speed of 40mph!

In 2001, the U.S. Government selected the first flight of the Wright Brothers as the image to be embossed on North Carolina's issue of the 25 cents coin.

The famous European traveler Marco Polo's journals record that in the 14th century, Chinese merchants used to launch kites with people tied to them. This was to see whether it was windy enough to set sail in their ships. If the kite did not fly, they stayed in port for another day.

THE 'WRIGHT' PUZZLE

Here's a fun way to help hunt down facts about the Wright Brothers. Solve the crossword with the help of the hints given below to get your facts 'Wright'!

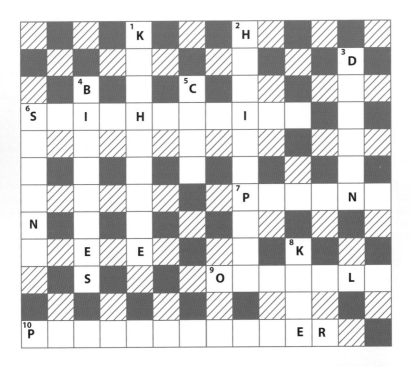

Down
1. _____ (9) was the name of their sister.
2. A toy that looked like a _____ (10) sparked the brothers' first interest in flying.
3. The Wright boys did most of their growing up in _____ (6), a town in Ohio.
4. In 1892, the brothers started a business repairing _____ (8).
5. A _____ (4) was used by the brothers to decide who would fly their new machine first.
6. Wilbur did not go to college because he was injured while playing _____ (6).
8. _____ (4) was the name of their first aeronautical experiment.

Across
6. _____ (11) is the museum which has preserved *The Flyer*.
7. The Wright brothers got a _____ (6) for their flying machines so that nobody could copy their ideas without their permission.
9. _____ (7) piloted the plane that flew for 12 seconds on December 17, 1903.
10. _____ (12) was the British inventor who first flew hand gliders in 1895.

Available now

Putting the fun back into readin

Explore the latest from Campfire at
www.campfire.co.in